Living LANGUAGE

LANGUAGE CHANGE

Shelley Martin

Hodder & Stoughton

A MEMBER OF THE HODDER HEADLINE GROUP

D0525853

Acknowledgements

Every effort has been made to trace copyright holders of material reproduced in this book. Any rights not acknowledged will be acknowledged in subsequent printings if notice is given to the publisher.

The author would like to thank Elizabeth Briggs at the West Yorkshire Archive Service, and her sister, Anne Baker, for her help in research.

To Matthew, James, Hannah and Steve, who had to do without me while I was doing this.

SHELLEY MARTIN

Orders: please contact Bookpoint Ltd, 39 Milton Park, Abingdon, Oxon OX14 4TD. Telephone: (44) 01235 400414, Fax: (44) 01235 400454. Lines are open from 9.00–6.00, Monday to Saturday, with a 24 hour message answering service. Email address: orders@bookpoint.co.uk

British Library Cataloguing in Publication Data
A catalogue record for this title is available from The British Library

ISBN 0 340 73087 0

First published 1999
Impression number   10 9 8 7 6 5 4 3 2 1
Year   2005 2004 2003 2002 2001 2000 1999

Cover photo from The Ronald Grant Archive
Typeset by Fakenham Photosetting Limited, Fakenham, Norfolk NR21 8NL
Printed in Great Britain for Hodder & Stoughton Educational, a division of Hodder Headline Plc, 338 Euston Road, London NW1 3BH by Scotprint Ltd, Musselburgh, Scotland.

Contents

1 Languagespotting

This chapter will:

- introduce you to the idea of language change
- give you ideas about how to find study materials yourself
- look at areas of language in which change has occurred
- give you examples of texts to study which show such changes.

The study of language change can be a terrifying experience for students. You are faced with armies of dates and terms which mean very little when taken out of context, and then confronted with concepts and ideas which seem impossible to grasp. What this book hopes to do is to give you a degree of independence in your language study, to empower you (there's a 1990s word already!) not only to notice and explore developments in language for yourself, but to find your own data to do it with. Perhaps a key thought to hold in your mind is that you are a sophisticated user of language and are beginning from an informed position about the topic. This gives you a firm platform from which to explore changes in language.

So, where should you start?

The first thing to do is to start using your eyes and ears. You live in a linguistic world, being bombarded from all directions by the spoken and written word. You turn on the radio when you wake up, you listen to your Walkman on the way to college, you yawn past shop signs on the bus, you go to the library to get a book for an essay, you eat chips for dinner, you cadge a lift home in your friend's parents' car, you watch Harry Enfield . . .

- . . . but did you notice that the DJ, perhaps Chris Evans, called people 'buddy'?
- . . . or that you got your Walkman out of its 'boogie bag'?
- . . . or that the record store was called *The Hip Hop Shop*, the computer supplier *Lasertronics*, the firework suppliers *The Pyropractors*?
- . . . did you notice that you did not in fact go to the library, you went to *The Learning Resource Centre*?
- . . . or that you were not eating chips but 'fries', according to the menu?
- . . . did you notice the brand name of the car? Was It a *Probe* or a *Twingo*?

■ ... did you notice the way Harry Enfield uses accents, eg Mr Cholmondley Warner with his old-fashioned received pronunciation, or RP (as on the *Mercury* adverts)?

You will probably know already that 'buddy' has various **connotations**. It is American in origin and has the obvious associations with Buddy Holly. It also is the term used for a supporter of an AIDS sufferer, a very close relationship indeed.

The *Walkman* is a word invented by Sony to name their product. It is possibly a compound of two nouns or the ellipted version of 'walk(ing) man'. Its 'boogie bag' is again a new term given to an old object to give it more appeal. It is alliterative and plays on 'boogie' meaning to dance.

The Hip Hop Shop uses alliteration and assonance for its impact and also cashes in on the name of a dance craze. *Lasertronics* is part compound (laser) and part blend (-tronics) and *The Pyropractor* is part derivation from *pyro* Greek for fire, and part blend using the end of chiropractor, from the Greek *praktikos* meaning practical or effective.

The use of *Learning Resource Centre* is part of a drive to rename things with negative or old-fashioned connotations, just as the person washing the supermarket floor had a badge on announcing that she was a 'Cleanliness Facilitator'. This is one aspect of **Political Correctness**, covered in more detail later in this chapter.

The chip issue is a big one. The influence on English from America is powerful and it is happening via the media: television, film, the Internet and computer programmes. 'Chip' has also picked up a second meaning. *The Chip Shop* could equally be the name of a computer store! There are many other examples if you keep your eyes and ears open. Have you been to the 'movies' or the 'cinema' lately? Do you pick up the 'mail' or the 'post'?

Brand names are a fertile area for language change and cars are no exception. *Probe* is usually used as a verb, but it has been 'converted' to a noun here with all its attendant connotations, which cash in on the sex appeal of a fast and sophisticated car. The *Twingo* is a coinage which makes the car sound fun but practical (two in and go?)

Lastly, Mr Cholmondley Warner shows us very clearly that the standard accent RP, which we tend to think of as fixed, is in fact, changing. The newsreader, Trevor MacDonald, does not sound like him!

If you regularly notice any features like these, you are well on the way to becoming a student of language change. They are all examples of how language is changing and adapting to the new demands placed on it by a developing society. Language is a powerful tool in society, used to express emotions, record events and information, tell others how to do things, to discuss topics and sometimes persuade others to our point of view. As those topics and events change, the language changes too. Without people and their activities, languages die. Latin, for example, was the spoken and written language of much of the civilised world under the Roman Empire, but it is not spoken in the 20th century, because its speakers retreated back from whence they came, taking their language with them.

All human activity involves contact of some kind and it is this contact which triggers off changes.

ACTIVITY 1

1 Make a list of all the words you can think of which show possible change in action, using examples like the ones above. Think about your average day and the activities you see and experience which could generate changes. A useful question to ask is if you would expect the word to appear in the dictionary. If the answer is no, there is a good chance you have hit on a valuable example. Some starting points might be:

- adverts on television and radio/billboards
- magazines, particularly music and fashion

- the speech of older people – listen to your grandparents!
- the speech of your contemporaries (**slang**) in the café or common room.

2 Now set up a 'language diary' which can be an old exercise book or note book and collect language examples. Bring them in for discussion next lesson. These form a valuable resource to use in exam answers and are far better than trotting out the ones from text books.

Become a language junkie

Apart from spotting language odds and sods, for systematic study, you need to handle larger texts. So where do you find them? Well, the following selection was gathered from old bookshelves, jumble sales and junk shops. One I found in an old farmhouse on holiday in Somerset! However, you need to be clear about what you are looking at in each case. Language works in a very complex way and there are different types of language change to be aware of. If you went to see a new band and you were assessing its success, you might rate it first in terms of the lyrics, then the meaning, then the effectiveness of the communication and then the presentation. Similarly, you must assess language by looking at its different component parts:

- the *words* (vocabulary or **lexis**)
- the *meaning* (**semantics**)
- the *grammar* (constructions used to carry the meaning)
- the *spelling* (**orthography**) and **graphology** (writing styles) in written texts
- the **phonology** in spoken texts.

Some linguists will categorise these differently, but as long as you look at the text with several different sets of eyes, you will find valuable material and keep your findings organised. For each of the following texts, let's look at the most obvious type of change first.

Lexis

Lexical change is spontaneous by nature because it keeps pace with inventions and technical developments in society. It is unpredictable and random and by far the most detectable form of language change. The 'shelf life' of new words varies enormously from days to centuries, depending on how successful the product is or how long the fashion lasts. There are some areas of life which have generated spectacular changes in lexis:

- technology
- fashion
- medicine
- food
- children's literature.

Technology

Perhaps the most fertile of these areas is technology. Consider this description of the state of communications technology from *The Children's Encyclopedia* edited by Arthur Mee in 1925. It describes the methods used to make the telegraph work automatically.

Many hundreds of pictures were telegraphed from Paris to London and from Manchester to London some years ago by a machine called the telectograph, an instrument invented by Mr Thorne Baker, and they were published each day in a London newspaper.

A banker in London can telegraph his signature to New York

Such machines may also be used to telegraph photographs of writing. A banker, for instance, can send his signature to an important document by wire, and thus save travelling perhaps from New York to London. All these wonderful inventions bring nations closer together, and make it possible to do business quickly over immense distances.

A still more romantic invention, which we may see brought to perfection, is the invention of television, or seeing from a distance. A German scientist named Ruhmer was actually able some years ago to see letters from a distance. If the letter A was held in front of a telegraph instrument, the letter A – that is an actual image of it – was seen at the same moment on a screen in some distant place.

The day when we shall see each other across space

When Ruhmer died he was making an instrument by which he hoped people would be able to see each other over the telegraph line while they were talking. The problem is very like that of telegraphing a picture, only the whole of the picture must be sent in a flash. Many inventors are working out a solution of this fascinating problem today, and it is humanly certain that seeing at a distance will be accomplished in due course.

The 'problem' certainly has been solved in the last 70 years or so and in the process has generated a multitude of lexical terms. If we compare the state of this area of technology with the 1990's equivalent, we will find a spectacular list of words unknown to Arthur Mee. Notice *telectograph*, which did not survive the lexical marathon to the present day, presumably because of the invention of the television. How many of the words in the section below will survive and for how long?

TEXT 1

PANASONIC 25" DOLBY PRO-LOGIC TV/VIDEO PACKAGE

TV

- *59cm Visible Screen Size – Fastext*
- *Auto Setup – Super Flat Picture Tube*
- *Digital Management System – Self Checks and*
- *Automatically Adjusts Picture Quality*
- *Supplied with Cabinet, 3D Bass Sub Woofer,*
- *Centre and Rear Speakers*

Video

- *4 Head Nicam Stereo Video Recorder*
- *Video+ and PDC – On Screen Displays*
- *Total Separate Selling Price: £999.98*
- *Dixons Deal: £979.00*

Panasonic is a brand name using *pan* from the Greek for 'all' and *sonic* from Latin meaning 'relating to audible sound'. *Dolby Pro-Logic* combines *pro* Latin for 'for' and *logic* as a computing term for something which carries out logical operations. You will have come across the **etymology** of *video* from the Latin 'to see', an oft-quoted example, but *Fastext* is **compound** using the adjective *fast* and the noun *text* but it has been blended together with the duplicate 't' lost through the process of **elision**. The Greek **prefix** (see **derivation**) *auto* meaning 'self' is often used in new formations and here it refers to the machine's ability to tune itself in and set its own clock. The *Sub Woofer* is an extra bass speaker to boost quality. *Sub* is again a Latin prefix meaning 'from below' and *woofer* uses the technique of **onomatopoeia** (the word is designed to sound like the sound) to demonstrate its effect. The word *speaker* to Arthur Mee would have meant a person who stands up to express an opinion. The **semantic shift** to a device to deliver sound in a music or TV system is obvious. Similarly, *head* as a part of the body is not the meaning here, but the spool round which the videotape runs. *Nicam* is a **coinage**. *Video +* combines word and symbol and *PDC* is an **acronym** for *Program Delivery Control*, a device to keep recording if your programme overruns (notice the American spelling of program not programme).

ACTIVITY 2

Work out the word formation processes in the following examples from the same catalogue, then find ten of your own. Check the glossary for word formation processes.

1 Bubblejet
2 LCD
3 Megabass
4 Surround sound
5 CD micro hi-fi (see **clipping**)
6 Internet
7 Multimedia PC
8 Gamepad
9 Mouse mat
10 Camcorder
11 Zoom (noun, as in digital zoom on a camera)
12 Palm pilot.

Fashion

Lexical change in fashion is very obvious, as it has to move and innovate to stay alive. The following extract from a pastoral drama, first performed in 1631, lists the fashion fancies of a Stuart lady.

Chains, coronets, pendants, bracelets and ear-rings;
Pins, girdles, spangles, embroyderies, and rings;
Shadowes, rebatoes, ribbands, ruffs, cuffs, falls,
Scarfes, feathers, fars, maskes, muffs, laces, cauls,
Thin biffaries, cobweb lawn, and fardingals,   5
Sweet fals, vayles, wimples, glasses, crisping pins,
Pots of ointment, combes, with poking sticks, and bodkines,
Coyfes, gorgets, fringes, rowles, fillets, and hair-laces,
Silks, damasks, velvets, tinsels, cloth of gold,
Of tissues with colours of a hundred fold   10
But in her tyres, so new fangled is she,
That which doth with her humour now agree,
Tomorrow she dislikes; now does she sweare
That a loose body is the neatest weare;
But ere an hour be gone she will protest   15
A straight gowne graces her proportion best;
Now in her hat, then in her hair is drest;
Now, of all fashions, she thinks change the best:
Nor in her weeds alone is she so nice
But rich perfumes she buys at any price;   20
Storax and spikenard she burns in her chamber,
And daubs herself with civet, musk and amber.

(English Women in Life and Letters, 1927)

The annual Paris fashion shows and the constant demand for 'this year's look' keeps an entire industry alive and demonstrate the need to change designs and consequently lexis. Clearly this was a priority in the 17th century too, as seen from the comment in line 18.

ACTIVITY 3

Using the full *Oxford English Dictionary* (OED), if you have access to it, or the nearest equivalent, list and find the meaning of all garments, materials and accessories mentioned in the extract above. Out of the full list (about 50) count how many you would use or wear today. You should find that it is very few.

Now consider this list of garments from *Cotton Traders* (1–9) and *Kayes* catalogue (10):

1 Pique – open-necked top made of cotton pique fabric
2 Interlock polo – same as a pique but made of cotton
3 Jogpants – fleecy casual trousers
4 Parka – hooded jacket for winter
5 Cheans – blend of chinos and jeans
6 Leggings – tight trousers usually elasticated
7 Body – body suit with fastener between the legs

8 Boxers – boxer shorts
9 Oxford – shirt
10 Scorts – **blend** of shorts and skirt.

None of these would have been used a decade ago and if we comp fabrics used by the Stuart lady – silk, damask, velvet, cloth of gold – wiu. those of today – lycra, polyester, elastane, ramie – we can clearly see the lexical development. Certain fashions are associated with different periods. In the 1920s women wore frocks, camibockers and boudoir caps. Young men wore plus fours and lounge suits. The 1940s saw twin sets, boleros and cloche hats. The 1960s was the age of the mini, the Chanel suit and disposable knickers, the 1970s unforgettable flares, platforms, kipper ties and the bubble perm. The 1980s brought grunge and the shell suit.... So, what have the 1990s to offer?

ACTIVITY 4

1 Sort the fashion words in the box below into the following categories:
   a garment
   b material
   c style
   d accessory (including footwear).

2 Using a range of fashion catalogues, add to the lists as many new terms as you can find. Comment on their linguistic features, formation and exact meanings. Feedback to the rest of the group and discuss your findings. Write them up in a report.

bootcut	suedette	thong	knee highs
sarong	cover up	twill	slub
jellies	stonewash	loafers	distressed
grandad	nehru	windbreaker	hold ups

Medicine

One very obvious area of development in this century has been medicine. Every day new strains of viruses emerge. New diseases are generated by random circumstances, for example, AIDS. Drug companies market the same basic drug under a variety of brand names to maximise sales, so: Paracetomal becomes Panadol, Disprol, Calpol, Hedex; Nicotine becomes Nicorette, Nicotinelle, Nicoril. Consider that penicillin was not discovered and developed by Alexander Fleming until 1928 and not commercially available until the Second World War. The status of medical research at the beginning of this century can be seen from this extract from *Mrs Beeton's Book of Household Management* published in 1912. It provides detailed instructions for the treatment of disease and illness.

Scarlet Fever

Most cases recover in a fortnight. Even the mild cases must be nursed, for there is no remedy which will cut short an attack. The patient must be put to bed and administered a milk diet. Hot flannel or cotton wool should be wrapped round the throat, and steam may be inhaled by the mouth when the throat is sore. A hot bath and purgatives must be given to remedy the kidney affection. During convalescence tonics should be administered, for which purpose quinine and iron are probably the best.

Anaemia

Remove the patient, if possible, from all influences that tend to injure the health. Have the teeth attended to, and if necessary, artificial teeth supplied. Change of air from the town to the country, or more particularly, to the seaside, is often beneficial, and cold sponging, especially with salt water, is also helpful. Iron may be given in the form of steel drops.

Asthma

Avoid everything likely to set up an attack, particularly indigestible articles of diet. During the attack, if there is reason to believe that the stomach is at fault, an emetic of powdered ipecacuanha, or sulphate of zinc may be given. Temporary relief may be obtained by the patient taking a few whiffs from a pipe of tobacco or stramonium. Joy's Cigares Anti-asthmatiques are useful. Change of air is often beneficial, and so are such tonics as cold sponging and the shower bath.

Syphilis

The health, in such cases, must be improved by a visit to the seaside, if possible, or a sea voyage, by liberal diet and regularity of living. Preparations containing iron and quinine are valuable, and may be given in conjunction with iodine of potassium.

Hysteria

The patient must be spoken to kindly, yet firmly, and be told to stop any eccentricities. Loosen the dress and remove anything tight from the neck. Give 1 teaspoonful of spirit of sal-volatile in water. If no heed is paid to what is said, dash cold water upon the face. Change of scene, cheerful society, physical exercise, and the cultivation of mental control are the best means of overcoming hysterical tendencies, especially the two latter means.

So, the actual treatments for the above complaints were:

- steam and tonic for scarlet fever;
- false teeth and a cold sponge down for anaemia;
- vomiting, a smoke and a cold swill down for asthma;
- potassium and good living for syphilis; and
- a brisk walk and a stern talking to for mental instability.

A quick overview of the drug lexis used by Mrs Beeton shows clear evidence of lexical change. Definitions of the drugs used:

- Quinine – a bitter alkaloid compound from cinchona barks used as a tonic and against fever. Now found in tonic water!
- Ipecacuana – extract of a South American creeping plant used as an emetic (ie to make you vomit).
- Zinc sulphate – obtained by the action of sulphuric acid on zinc, used as an astringent and emetic.
- Iodine of potassium – used as an antiseptic.
- Stramonium – a drug from a narcotic plant, used to treat asthma.
- Sal-volatile – ammonium carbonate used as a 'smelling salt'.

Lexically, there is very little here which is familiar, although many of the basic ingredients are still used in modern drugs in a modified form. Since this time, the lexis of the world of chemistry has exploded. We are all familiar with antibiotic names – Amoxycillin, Ampicillin, Erythromycin, Streptomycin, Co-tromoxazole, Chloramphenicol. These are perhaps the most familiar drugs in use in the 20th century. Mrs Beeton would also be unfamiliar with asthma treatments such as antihistamines, bronchodilators and corticosteroids, and anti-depressants for psychiatric disorders leading to hysteria, such as Venaflaxine, Nefazodone and Trazodone.

The most worrying result of the chemical explosion this century has been the rise of the culture of drug abuse. Aldous Huxley signalled the nightmare vision of a drug-controlled population in *Brave New World* with his imaginary 'soma'. With the proliferation of mind-altering substances now available his vision could be said to have come true. Along with the chemical names for new drugs, there has also sprouted a fertile crop of alternative **slang** names, another aspect of lexical development.

ACTIVITY 5

1 Go to your local chemist and make a list of products' names from the items on the shelves. Look at the **morphology** of the words and see if you can find any patterns. For example, many asthma drugs have elements such as *vent* as in Maxivent and Ventolin because they work by opening the passages in the lungs. Many products for women begin with *fem* as in Feminax (for menstrual pain) and Femodene (an oral contraceptive). Collect data individually and pool them as a group. This could lead to many areas for investigations.

2 It may be helpful to consider this extract from a book by Carl Ackerman about George Eastman in 1906 about the coinage of the brand name *Kodak*. (Eastman is the father of the late Linda McCartney and the founder of the Kodak camera empire.) It demonstrates some of the criteria employed by companies when trying to market their products:

Eastman was determined that this product should have a name that could not be mis-spelled or mis-pronounced, or infringed or copied by anyone. He wanted a strong word that could be registered as a trademark, something that everyone would remember and associate only with the product … K attracted him. It was the first letter of his mother's family name. It was 'firm and unyielding'.

It was unlike any other letter and easily pronounced. Two k's appealed to him more than one, and by a process of association and elimination he originated *kodak* and gave a new name to a new commercial product. The trademark was registered in the United States Sept. 4, 1888.

(As quoted in *A History Of English*, B. Strang)

Apply these criteria to your drug names and add others, which you think have been used in their creation. Note that phonological effect was very important to Eastman, as Kodak was a comparatively rare, true coinage. There are other factors to take into account as suggested earlier.

Suggestion – this approach could be widened into a study of brand names for any product. For example, perfumes, cereals, chocolate bars etc.

3 Complete the chart on page 10 by going out and interviewing other young people about the terms they have heard used for non-medical drugs. The group and chemical name is supplied for you. You are looking for the slang terms for each, another facet of the chemical/lexical explosion this century. One is 'completed' as an example. This could be developed into an investigation.

Drug Name	L.S.D. (Lysergic Acid)	Cannabis	Ecstasy (MDMA)	Heroin	Cocaine / Crack
Effect	Hallucinogen	Hallucinogen	C.N.S. Stimulant	C.N.S. Stimulant	C.N.S. Stimulant
Examples of Slang names	Acid Trips Tabs Haze Microdots Lysergide				

C.N.S. = Central Nervous System

Food

English has always borrowed widely from other languages but one specific area of current lexical change is that of food. There are many reasons for this, but probably the most important one is that we are much more widely travelled and more cosmopolitan than our forebears. A word will enter the lexis if there is a need for it and, most importantly, if there has been contact with the word in question. Twentieth century speakers have access to language from all over the globe via the media and foreign travel. Most people have travelled abroad or have watched the numerous cookery programmes from Madhur Jaffrey to Ken Hom, and are familiar with the ingredients and the terms being used. Large supermarkets now stock a range of products unheard of when Mrs Beeton was writing such as balsamic vinegar, sun-dried tomatoes and marscapone. In her *Book of Household Management* (1912), there is a clear indicator of one area of change in food habits, as she writes only 27 pages out of 2000 on vegetarian cookery, and remarks,

From the earliest ages the doctrines and practices of vegetarianism have been observed from necessity, as a religious duty, or on the grounds of health ... In England the question has come to the front on the grounds of dietetic reform, and a number of persons known as 'Vegetarians' abstain from animal food altogether.

This is clearly an alien concept to Mrs Beeton and vegetarian staples such as pulses, soya and tofu do not appear in the book. To cater for this social change, language has adapted by integrating terms for ingredients from other cultures. Many of the words we take for granted now as everyday food and drink are, in fact, borrowings. For example, *coffee* was originally an Arabic word *qahwah* adapted in Turkish as *kahve* then to Italian as *caffè* and subsequently to American and British English, where it is now regarded as part of the culture.

ACTIVITY 6

1 With the help of a good dictionary, track down the origin of the food words in the box below. It would be useful to mark the results on a world map, if possible, pooling your findings as a group, to demonstrate the range of sources we borrow from.

casserole	paprika
sushi	fromage frais
tea	chilli con carne
yoghurt	pitta bread
balti	sangria
feta	moussaka
scampi	pistachio
cappuccino	korma
hashbrowns	smorgasbord
cous-cous	stirfry

2 Study as many cookbooks as you can and scour them for borrowed words. If possible, trace their origins using a quality dictionary. Again, this will generate many ideas for investigations and projects. For example, you could trace the rate of **borrowings** from Empire countries as we have a large number from former colonies such as India. Some, like coffee, are related to the former trade routes and would be fascinating to investigate. More simply, you could examine the stock at a large supermarket and assess the range of foods and their origins. The possibilities are endless.

Children's literature

Writers are creative and it is the nature of the job to engage interest and entertain. The old master of creative lexis was perhaps Lewis Carroll, author of the Alice books. An accomplished mathematician, he wrote his books to entertain Alice Liddell, a friend's daughter. On a deeper level, he explores the nature of language in all aspects, one of which is word formation. This is seen clearly in *Jabberwocky* from *Through The Looking Glass*:

Twas brillig, and the slithy toves
Did gyre and gimble in the wabe:
All mimsy were the borogroves,
And the mome raths outgrabe.

What does he mean by *brillig*? Is it a blend of brilliant and something else? Is *slithy* slithery and slimy? The intention is to push language to change, to invigorate it with new vocabulary and so broaden its use and range of meaning. One of Carroll's coinages which has survived is *chortle* listed in the *Reader's Digest Universal Dictionary* (1987) as:

Chortle – n. A snorting, joyful chuckle. (Blend of CHUCKLE and SNORT, coined by Lewis Carroll.)

A more recent writer who experimented with lexis was Roald Dahl. Look at this passage from *The BFG*. In it, the giant is introducing Sophie to the delights of his drink, *frobscottle*.

changes are dependent on use and the people who employ language creatively, as discussed in the previous section.

When a word shifts its meaning, it can move towards a more positive one – a process known as **amelioration** – or a negative one – **pejoration**. *Crap* is an example of pejoration and the popular *wicked* to mean wonderful is an example of amelioration. Words can also move to cover a wider meaning, **broadening**: my students assure me that that *slag* applies to both sexes now! What a relief to have one abusive word for women which is multi-purpose!

There are over 2000 abusive terms, many of which have pejorated from a harmless starting point. For example, *hussy* from housewife and *slag* from the residue of ore smelting. Conversely, words can limit their meaning, **narrowing**. For example, *function* has always had a very broad meaning of 'a purpose' but now seems to be narrowing to the specific functions of computerised equipment, as a scan through any recent manual will demonstrate. The Old English *deor* originally meant any beast but when the French word *animal* was borrowed, *deor* narrowed to the modern *deer*.

If you follow a word right back to its source, that is, the original meaning, you are studying **etymology** – the study of the derivation of words. Knowing the etymology of a word is fascinating but it can lead people to take prescriptive attitudes to meaning, insisting that the original should be adhered to. This clearly goes against the basic principles of language change. Consider this letter to the *Sunday Telegraph* in June 1994:

A television newsreader referred recently to the 'enormity of the international rescue operation'. What is so 'monstrously wicked' (OED) about saving people's lives?

Peter Wardle, Kidderminster

This emphasis on the correctness of the original meaning can also lead to false etymology in which the origin is incorrectly quoted eg *avocado* from *ahuacatl* (Aztec) to 17th century Spanish *aguacate*. It became popularised by confusion with Spanish *avocado* (advocate) ie a wealthy person who could afford legal help. Even Dr Johnson is thought to have mistaken the etymology of *island*, thinking it to be derived from Latin *insula*, when in fact it is from the Anglo Saxon *iland*. The 's' was actually inserted in the 17th century by the Bishop of Cambridge to make the word look more like the Latin. Another example of this is *whore*, which acquired the 'w' by analogy, but in fact, derives from the Anglo Saxon, *hore*.

ACTIVITY 8

Using a good etymological dictionary, look up the origins of these words:

1 barbecue
2 buxom
3 cabaret
4 camisole
5 gay
6 hospital
7 jerkin
8 blouse
9 purple
10 streak
11 trigger
12 wallet

Political correctness

One area of semantic change, which has caused many new words and phrases to be generated, is **political correctness**. Thought by some to be a pernicious form of censorship, it is seen by its promoters as a search for a more caring language. Born out of American university campuses in the mid 1980s, it seeks to rid the lexicon of words and phrases which betray principally racial, sexual and ableist thinking, such as *blacks, birds* and *spastics*. It has affected thinking radically with people wondering whether to use terms such as 'it's a black and white issue', or how to refer to partners. Many other -isms have jumped on the bandwagon such as heightism, ageism and alphabetism (discrimination against people whose names are at the end of the alphabet). As with all language change, the attitudes are reflected in the language. Consider this statement from Enid Blyton's *Chimney Corner Stories* (1963):

She wouldn't play with the golliwog because she said he ought to wash himself, and get himself white. . . .

The word *golliwog* was coined by Bertha Upton for a series of children's books at the end of the last century and is now so negatively connotated that it is rarely seen. Mrs Beeton speaks of the 'housewife' being 'the mistress of the household' and the duties of the 'hostess'. These three words have all changed in meaning.

ACTIVITY 9

1 How have *housewife, mistress* and *hostess* changed their meaning? How would you use them today?

2 Discuss the following statements from older texts. How have attitudes changed in each case and how is that reflected in the language?

■ Betsy May went out of the shop, looking backwards at the beautiful kitchen stove. She had never wanted anything so much in all her life.
> (*Tales of Betsy May,* Enid Blyton, 1940)

■ Many brains of famous men have been examined . . . The contrast is very great between them and the brains of such a humble type of mankind as the Bushman of South Africa.
> (*Children's Encyclopedia,* Arthur Mee)

■ Cretins are ugly dwarfed idiots
> (*The New Illustrated Universal Reference Book,* 1933)

■ In diagnosing hysteria from genuine disease, the chief points are: that although the person may fall in a faint or be seized with convulsions she does not bite her tongue or hurt herself . . .
> (as above)

■ History, strictly speaking, we are told, has only to do with man as a human being: and indeed in ordinary talk we limit its scope to the two thousand years during which he has left a conscious record of his thoughts and actions.
> (as above)

■ They only knew that Will was bad, and had been whipped.
> (*The Put-em Rights,* Enid Blyton, 1946)

■ Doctors in the hospitals find out about the patients' illnesses. Then the doctors tell the nurses what to do to help the patients get better.
[accompanied by pictures of doctors (all male) and nurses (all female)].
> (*The Nurse,* Vera Southgate, 1963)

3 Research the issues of political correctness using articles, textbooks, CD-ROMs and discussion. Pool your findings and write an article for a broadsheet newspaper (eg 'Comment' in the *Guardian*) putting a firm view on the issue. You must argue

Conquest of 1066. When it emerged from its chrysalis in the works of Chaucer, mutated into a new hybrid form, Caxton recorded it using his astute business brain, his newly imported printing crafts and his translating skills. He fretted constantly about his choice of terms and expressions from all the dialects on offer, and hoped that they would 'be understonden of the redars and herers'. But by doing this, he began to make literature accessible to a wide range of people and created, as much as anyone, a fixed form of written English, creating a memorable milestone in its history. The spoken word went on and did its own thing, but the new generations of printers who took over from Caxton made sure that the written word did as it was told – the London way.

'Farewell, farewell to my beloved language,
Once English, now a vile orangutanuage'
(Ogden Nash)

Another aspect of standardisation is prescriptive attitudes. People have always held such views, but at certain points in history, they became hot political potatoes. Long before Caxton's time, comments were passed about the varieties of English on offer as opposed to the fixed simplicity of the Latin. A Cornishman, John of Trevisa, while translating another man's work in 1385, could not stop himself from snapping irritably:

Englischmen ... by commyxstion and mellyng furst wiþ Danes and afterward wiþ Normans, in menye contray longage ys apeyred [*corrupt*] and som use strange wlaffyng, chyteryng, harryng and garryng, grisbytting.

He was more specific in one case with a southerner's familiar contempt for all things northern ...

Al the longage of the Nor humbres, and specialych at York, ys so scharp, slyttyng, and unschape, at we Southeron men may that longage unnethe undurstonde.

The idea of *apeyred* (corrupt) language is still with us, as can be seen from the prescriptive statements of the National Curriculum, which require students to speak standard English to pass with a grade C. Dialectal speech alone will get you nowhere in life today – you must be able to switch to 'correct' English if you want the job. Ever present between Caxton's press and now, **prescriptivism** rose to a memorable peak in the 18th century with the call for a language Academy in 1712 by Jonathan Swift, so that there might be, 'Ways found to fix it forever'. This was followed by Samuel Johnson's Dictionary in 1755 and the highly prescriptive grammar books of Robert Lowth and Lindley Murray in 1762 and 1799.

'A harmless drudge'

Out of this need for a fixed form came the dictionaries and standardisation of spelling and meaning. In 1582, Richard Mulcaster, a headmaster, wrote a list of 7,000 English words and how to spell them. Early dictionaries were limited to glossaries and lists of hard words such as Richard Cawrey's

Table Alphabeticall in 1604 containing 2,500 'hard usuall English wordes', aimed at 'Ladies, Gentlewomen, or any other unskilfull persons'. This got the dictionary ball rolling and led to the milestone of Johnson's *A Dictionary of the English Language* with 40,000 entries. Serious dictionary as it was, it was very individual with biased entries and personal comments as it was the work of one man, who defined a lexicographer (dictionary maker) as 'a harmless drudge'. It was not until 1879 that a truly objective and unbiased edition emerged, to become the *Oxford English Dictionary* (*OED*). Now spelling is well and truly fixed and reinforced by a catalogue of specialist dictionaries, television shows such as *Countdown*, and the weekly spelling test in school, source of many a stomach ache on a morning.

Recap

Standardisation has affected language in all its departments.

- **Lexis** – prescriptive attitudes have stopped some words being adopted eg the battle over 'inkhorn' terms in the 18th century. Johnson thought *skunk, mob* and *babble* offensive. Although dating from the sixteenth century, *fuck* only gatecrashed the dictionary party in 1936, after being bounced out for centuries. H. W. Fowler commented on 'ugly formations', in this case, a French borrowing:

The very special ugliness of *beaurocracy* is due to the way its mongrel origin is flaunted in our faces by the telltale syllable -eau-; it is to be hoped that formations in this respect may be avoided.

(*The King's English*, 1908)

- **Semantics** – dictionaries fixed meanings, leading to people not accepting new uses, as shown in this comment quoted in *A History of English* by Barbara Strang:

Sir, – Every so often a familiar word takes on a new and senseless life. Superb, for instance, is now commonly abused.

- **Grammar** – printing and prescriptivism made sure that certain rules stuck, even though they were often illogically based on Latin and Greek models. For example, you can't split infinitives because you can't in Latin. Illogical, Captain Kirk – infinitives have always been split in English.

- **Spelling** – printing and dictionaries fixed spellings and led to the idea of correct versions. Before printing and for some time after, people spelt as they spoke, including Shakespeare, who wrote his own name several different ways. Robert Burchfield sums it up:

'... written English has remained relatively static since the invention of printing about the middle of the 15th century, but spoken English ... has changed repeatedly since then'.

(from *The English Language*)

- **Graphology** – before printing, scribes produced written manuscripts using house styles, depending on where they had been trained. After

| 1980s | The National Curriculum demanded standard English and spelling skills for GCSE grade C. |
| 2000 | See Activity 12. |

ACTIVITY 12

What do you think will happen to English in the new millenium? What events or inventions can you predict which will affect lexis, spelling, meaning, grammar and graphology? (Consider computers which write as you speak into them, international videophones or translating machines.) Start by looking at a range of sci-fi material and see what they have done with language: *Red Dwarf*, *Star Trek*, Terry Pratchett.

Back to the future

All this history is background information to allow you to make *informed* comments about texts. Examining boards do not set texts before the 16th century. However, you would be expected to refer to these historical events as they created the English you will be analysing. In Chapter 1, you began to spot texts from language around you. Now you need to extend that to a wider range of styles and ages. The text on page 29 is from the Huddersfield Archive. Archives contain a treasure trove of material, which are locally based (and therefore interesting) and very cheap. Some archives are attached to the local library and some are separate, but there will be one somewhere near you. Documents of all kinds are stored from diaries and letters to official records. Analysis of texts like these will help you in many areas of A-Level study such as data questions, essay answers on language change, stylistic analysis, investigations and coursework. All you need to do is find out from your library service if they have an archive or where the nearest one is and go and tell the archivist what you want. You will be doing ground-breaking research on your own and doing it with attitude!

Tarts for tea, Henry

The charming text on pages 29 and 30 is the plan of a table setting for the 21st birthday of Henry Beaumont of the Whitley estate, between Leeds and Huddersfield, which his family had owned since the Middle Ages. He was the son of Richard and Susanna, one of 15 children. Richard died in 1723 and Susanna in 1730 so he actually inherited the estate when he was only seven. He was probably thoroughly spoilt as a result. The plan may have been written by the housekeeper, or trustee. A brief scan shows that the spelling is far more standardised than the 15th century ones above by Caxton and John of Tevisa. However, it is certainly not fully regular, as in a modern text, but it is clearly at the later end of the period between 1500 and 1750 (Johnson's dictionary was published in 1755) with many foreign borrowings such as *pistachio, ragout* and *Spanish cream*. The actual date was 1738.

TEXT 5 ▶

The Dinner at Whitley Hall 18th Dec.t 1738 when Henry Beaumont Esq.r came of Age ——;

A Ragou'd Breast of Veal

A Gravy Soop remov'd with Turbot again with a Pheasant & Snipes

Litle Chickens boiled

Almond Cheesecakes

A White fricasee of Sweetbreads

Oysters in Scalop Sholls

Preserved Oranges

Jelly's

Almond Butter

Pistachio Nuts

A Pyramid of wet & dry sweetmeats with a preserved Pineapple Green.

Spanish Cream

Leach

Sylabubs

Preserved Damsons

Woodcocks

Roasted Turkey

Lemon Posset in a Large glass Bason

Roasted Tongues

A Haunch of Venison removed with Wild Ducks.

2 raised mince Pies

A large Jole of Sturgeon

Lobsters

A Cods Head removed with Lucca Olives

Sago Pudding

Fricasee of Potatoes

Lemon Posset in a large glass Bason

A Goose

Partridges

Almond Cheesecakes

Stewed Apples green

Jelly's

Lemon Jelly

A Pyramid of wet & dry Sweetmeats

Leach

Chocolate Cream

China Oranges

Preserved Damsons

Fricasee of Rabbits brown

Hogs Cheek

Tarts

Boiled Turkey

A Pease Soop removed with a Venison Pasty again with Veal

Scotch Collops

ACTIVITY 13

In groups, translate the foods onto a large diagram, then confer with others to see if you agree. Next, write down any differences you can see between this and a modern text. Try to group them under the headings given below.

- **Lexis** (look up syllabubs, damsons, posset, sweetbreads, leach, etc)
- **Semantics** (do tarts, sole and basin still mean the same thing?)
- **Grammar** (stewed apples green?)

- **Spelling** (so many to choose from!)
- **Graphology** (look at those capitals!)

You will need access to a good dictionary which gives etymological references. Try to relate your findings to historical knowledge and suggest *why* these changes have come about. Remember there is no correct answer – your suggestion is as valid as anyone else's as this text has not been studied before, so get out there and chart some unknown territory.

Spot the Differences!

These are some of the comments of a new group of students which show how skilled they are at spotting evidence of language change.

Lexis

- Some **obsolete** words used like *haunch* and *leach* (see glossary).
- Unusual lexis describing foods we no longer eat such as *snipes, sweetbreads* (calf's pancreas or thymus gland), *sweetmeats* and *posset.*
- *Collop* is a regional word meaning a slice of meat or fish, still used in the Yorkshire area.
- *ragou'd* is here used as a verb whereas it is normally a noun – a **conversion**.
- Archaic words like *removed* meaning 'replaced by'.
- Much foreign influence and imported foods, such as: *fricassee, pistachio, olives, Spanish cream.*

Semantics

- There has been a shift in the word *sole* – here refers to fillet of sturgeon whereas now it is a specific fish. Is this a **narrowing** of meaning?
- *basin* seems to be a decorative bowl here – we would use a basin for more functional purposes, not on a fancy table setting.

Grammar

- There are some examples of **inverted syntax**: *pineapple green, rabbits brown, apples green* and *little chickens boiled.*
- We would not use the past participle ending on *roast/ed turkey.*

Spelling

- Many variant spellings are used such as *soop* (soup), *sylabub* (syllabub), *fricasee* ('fricassee', a French borrowing), *escalop* (scallop), *remov'd* with the apostrophe of elision not used today for a past tense ending.

■ The writer uses unfamiliar letters: the long 's' in *frica∫see*.
■ The apostrophe is used for the plural in *jelly's*.

Graphology

■ The graphology is ornate and makes the text hard to read especially in the initial capitals *P, L, V* and *R*.
■ The capital *A* is formed like a lower case letter.

COMMENTARY

This was written before Johnson's Dictionary but there were some at hand to help the scholar. In 1721 Nathaniel Bailey published his *Universal Etymological English Dictionary*, which contained 28,000 entries, was widely used and may well have been in the Beaumont household. However, the idea of the spelling *mistake* had still not fully taken root and there were many variants used in the writings of even well-educated people, so this text would by no means be considered to be full of errors – just individual style! At this time, George II of Hanover, was on the throne, father of Prince George of *Blackadder* fame, whose madness was the subject of the award-winning film *The Madness of King George*. The slave trade was very well established and England was becoming a major colonial power with many new colonies overseas, to add to the well developed communities on the eastern seaboard of America. The huge variety of fish, meats and game shows a marked difference in eating habits from now – no vegetarian options here. The wealth of the family is clearly indicated with foods imported from the Empire, like sago, olives and pistachio nuts. Sago has obviously gone downmarket since then.

ACTIVITY 14

1 Write the menu you would like for your 18th birthday buffet (clock the posh French borrowing in this statement). Construct an investigation to compare the foods on offer with Henry Beaumont's. Consider the range, the ingredients, the origins of the items. Also look at the way in which the items are described. Your findings should cover lexis, semantics, grammar and spelling.
2 Write an imaginary account of Henry Beaumont's celebrations as a coursework piece. You may have to do some further research on dress and entertainment etc.
3 Examine the extract from the diary of Richard Tolson on page 33 from 1785, 47

years after Henry's 21st. This again is from the Huddersfield Archive and shows how this material brings people from the past alive for us, making the study of *living language* so enjoyable and relevant. He was obviously impressed by Amsterdam's night life! So, what's changed? There is a transcript after the diary extract to help you.

Answer the following question, using the diary extract and the transcript:

■ How has English changed since the early eighteenth century? Your answer should cover lexis, semantics, grammar, spelling and graphology.

TEXT 6 TRANSCRIPT OF RICHARD TOLSON'S DIARY – October 16 1785

There is 80 p(e)r Cent duty on flower in Holland a publican who buys 18 Gall(on)s of small beer at Ams(terdam) which cost only 2 florins the 18 Gall(on)s pays 27 Stuyvers duty – on entering his house – The above duty is the same on strong beer as small – – 15 p(e)r Cent duty is paid on all kinds of Meat in Holland – persons are Employd – who go about dayly to examine the Butchers Stalls etc – in order to take an account of the same – Every Chaldron of Coals or 38 Bushels – pays £8.10 duty, and d(itt)o of Turf is nearly the same – for 1 Maid servant a Tax is paid annually ab(ou)t £8–9 – & 3 d(itt)o cost ab(ou)t £42 in Holland – The Speeldhouses are permitted by the State by Licence – and pay a certain Sum yearly for each Girl that is maintained by them – they open ab(ou)t 10 oClo(ck) in the Ev(enin)g – when a number of them Sit on benches – exposed to publick view – all painted – like a Sett of dolls – and they are very Lewd Musick plays during the Evening – and the Girls dance with any person who goes there – there are a great number at Amsterdam.

This text shows the need for people to record their lives and experiences, either for themselves or for others, leaving a permanent record for future students of life and language like us. The circumstances in which they find themselves going through that process will obviously affect the product, as you will see in the next chapter.

Summary

In this chapter, you have :

- learnt about standardisation, including major figures and events
- explored changes in a real text with the help of a commentary
- explored changes in a real text independently.

and engage the French but they have always got the worst of it, the French and English soldiers are most excellent well it is a splendid army is the French army because they are so numerous, I wonder that they have an army of one hundred thousand men out here now and fifty thousand more they are I hear expecting soon from France, we are expecting a large reinforcement soon to arive from India and other places. We keep cracking away from our entrenchments at the Russians & think we shall have a general engagement with them outside yet before the town is taken, I wish the war was over and gentle peace returning, although I have not to go into it, yet it is dreadful to see so many men laying dead and wounded. The weather is beginning to be warm here again after a dismal, dreary long winter. I think I have no more news for you this time but perhaps by the time I write again I shall be able to tell of the fall of Sebastopol

please to remember me to father and give my respects to James and Martha and to all inquiring friends and believe me

I remain yours truly

John Land

9th Fusiliers

ACTIVITY 15

■ Read the letter and record your reactions to it. Discuss, as a whole group, the purpose, audience and tone.
■ Now write a modern, Standard English version in the appropriate tone and formality.

■ In groups, find where the differences occur between the language used by John and your modern versions. Classify the differences under appropriate headings (lexis, semantics and so on.)

Spot the differences

So, what have you found? The points below are those made by a group of about 15 students. See how they compare to yours. They are in no particular order.

■ There are some variant spellings, *addres* (address), *buisness* (business), *ingage* (engage), *supose* (suppose) Interestingly enough, *business* and *suppose* figure very highly in the list of words most frequently misspelt by A-Level students today, so the problems clearly are deeply rooted in the etymology and development of the words themselves.
■ There are very few full stops but capitals are in the expected places. Hyphens and commas are present.
■ The graphology is elaborate and hard to read in places.
■ The colloquial expression *cracking away* seems oddly out of place. It sounds old fashioned now.
■ There are some unusual grammatical constructions eg 'The French and English soldiers agree most excellent'.
■ It is very formal and distanced in tone even though it is to a family member.
■ He appears to be trying hard to write more formally than you would expect to his mum. It is almost as if it has been written by someone else and contains no personal details.
■ There is no address phrase at the top like 'Dear Mother'.
■ Some over formal language eg:
    'Please to remember me to father'
    'Never enjoyed better health than what I do at present'
    'I shall be able to tell of the fall of Sebastopol'
    Words like *numerous* and *engagement*.

Once you have overviewed the text and put it into historical context, you need to channel your findings and explore the points made. Start to draw some conclusions, so that the result begins to look like a systematic analysis of the data. Here is one suggested outline plan.

COMMENTARY **Introduction** – The letter was written at a point when the standardisation process was well on its way. It comes after the Johnson dictionary and the grammars of Lowth and Murray though before the introduction of universal education in 1870. Nevertheless, you would expect to find grammar and spelling largely in line with the modern versions. The cursive, joined up style of the writer suggests a school training with standard techniques for connecting words (ligatures in correct positions). John

A Few Plain Questions Answered

This poster was produced for the 1807 General Election, for the Yorkshire county constituency. It was dubbed the 'Great Yorkshire Election' and was the first contested Yorkshire election for 66 years. The three candidates for two seats were:

- William Wilberforce, known for his anti-slavery campaign
- Henry Lascelles, second Earl of Harewood
- Viscount Milton, only 21 at the time.

The election was remembered for the scandalous sums of money spent by the candidates, who routinely paid for their voters to travel to York, where the polling station was. Voting was public and so bribery and intimidation were common. Out of the three, Wilberforce and Milton were elected in a close-run contest and poor Lascelles, having spent over £100,000, (equivalent to approximately £7,000,000 now!), failed to win a seat. This poster is an attack on him by Milton's supporters. It takes the form of a series of questions and answers, with part one praising Milton and attacking Lascelles and part two also praising Milton's father Lord Fitzwilliam. Lascelles did reply with a similar poster entitled *A Few Plain Questions ANSWERED AS THEY OUGHT TO BE* (although it didn't get him very far).

ACTIVITY 24

1 In pairs, read aloud the questions and answers. Experiment with the tone and see which works best.
2 'Translate' the questions into modern standard English (see below for help).
3 In groups, list the differences between this and a modern text. Group your points under headings of your own choice.

Notes

- Wilberforce's bill to abolish slavery in the West Indies had just been passed in February 1807.

- Melville was Henry Dundas, Viscount Melville and First Lord of the Admiralty. Trotter was a civil servant in his service who had been accused of misusing funds.
- The Black Rod is and was an official of the House of Commons.
- A Freeholder was a person eligible to vote because he held freehold land to the value of 40 shillings a year.
- The King was George III.

Spot the Differences

Compare your findings with those below. This is a challenging text, which does require some background knowledge. There are, however, many fascinating features to be found, just by looking closely at the text.

Graphology

The most immediately striking feature is the odd 's' (long 's'), which is very different to our modern conventional one (short 's'). There is no immediately obvious pattern to their use except that short 's' seems to be used more at the beginnings of words (initial position) when capitalised. A variety of typefaces are used for emphasis.

Spelling

The use of capital letters is very varied with many nouns having them and some words all in capitals for emphasis. Spelling in line with modern versions, as this was written well after the Johnson dictionary, presumably by well educated, well read politicians.

Lexis

There are some unfamiliar words: *stealers* for thieves, *orator* for speaker and *freeholder* (see above). The obsolete word *peculator* means one who embezzles money. The lexis is loaded with emotive overtones (*bleeding Africa*) and semantic fields of deception and conflict. It is also very formal with archaic words such as *whence,* and Latinate vocabulary (*orator, despise, villify, deceptions*). The figurative serpent which Milton would have his reader strangle adds to the emotiveness of the text and has biblical overtones, all adding to its persuasive force.

Grammar and syntax

The grammar is very formal with long complex sentences involving a great deal of subordination. The interrogative sentences are often complex but answered by short noun phrases. The syntax is old-fashioned, for example, *Part First* where we would use Part One or First Part. There is a variant verb ending now obsolete in *delighteth.*

COMMENTARY This text is one of many forged in the furnace of political conflict and is designed to attack. The tone of the piece is aggressive, as you would expect from warring politicians. No holds are barred in the attempt to score points off the opponent, with inferences of religious persecution, financial mismanagement, poor speaking skills and dubious family connections. The points are highly selective and largely unsupported. Take, for example, the question about Lascelles' family. The answer given by his attackers is that he comes from a 'Family nobody knows'. On the reply poster, *A Few Questions Plain ANSWERED AS THEY OUGHT TO BE,* his supporters pronounce that he comes from 'one of the most ancient Families in the County ... who Fought for their King and Country under the Plantagenets, many Hundreds Years before the Family Of Fitzwilliam had a foot of land in the County'. Who are we to believe? The simple answer is that you believe who you want to believe because this material is not informative, it is a partial jigsaw with many missing pieces, designed to reinforce opinions already formed, and persuade those still wavering, by fair means or foul.

ACTIVITY 25

1 Try to write the reply poster *A Few Plain Questions ANSWERED AS THEY OUGHT TO BE.* Use the small sample given as a starting point. Try to keep the lexis, grammar and formality in line with this one. You are a supporter of Lascelles and you are attacking Milton and his father Lord Fitzwilliam. These would make an impressive wall display. Make sure you have access to quality dictionaries and a resource centre for further research.

TEXT 17

A few Plain Questions

ANSWERED AS THEY OUGHT TO BE.

· · · · ·

Ques. 14.   Whence is LASCELLES descended?

Answer.   From one of the most ancient Families in the County; their Names appear in the Records of Yorkshire in A. D. 1260; they represented Northallerton, when the Borough was first erected; and Fought for their King and Country under the Plantagenets, many Hundred Years before the Family of Fitzwilliam had a Foot of Land in the County.

2 Do an analysis of the use of long 's' and short 's' in Text 16. Ask yourself:

■ Where are they used? At the beginnings, middles or ends of words?
■ What happens with double 's'?
■ Does capitalisation affect the use?

Present your findings in graph form and write a list of conclusions about the use of the long 's' in this period. When you have done this, refer to the section below.

3 Tape BBC's *Question Time* and analyse the way the politicians answer the questions (use your discourse analysis skills). What similarities do you find with the question/answer device used on the poster?

The long 's' – the linguistic lowdown

1 Before 1800, most printers used two, lower case (small) 's' forms, known as long 's' and (wait for it) short 's'.

2 Long 's' was born in ancient Rome in their cursive (joined up) writing and was preserved by scribes in the ages which followed. Both can be seen in the Lindisfarne Gospels in the 7th century.

3 By the 12th century, each letter had found a niche, long 's' used for beginnings and middles of words and short 's' at the ends.

4 This trend was picked up by the printers and and lasted until the end of the 18th century.

5 Long 's' overlaps adjacent letters in combinations such as sh/st/si/ss (find the examples in the poster), which meant that printers had to make special types for them.

6 The man who finally terminated long 's' was Frenchman, Francoise-Ambroise Didot. He developed a new typestyle called 'modern face' and long 's's services were no longer required. It was now redundant, as there were two letters doing the same job and it was expensive to keep all the types needed.

7 Using the new typestyle, London printer John Bell published his newspaper *The World* in 1787 with not a long 's' in sight. Its days were numbered, as other printers quickly followed his lead. He said in the preface to his *Shakespeare* in 1788 that he wanted to make the lines more 'open' and avoid confusion with the letter 'f'.

8 The combined long and short 's' survives in the German Esszett (β)

Enforcing the peace

> Get the thing straight once and for all: the policeman isn't there to create disorder. The policeman is there to preserve disorder.
>
> (Richard Daley, Mayor of Chicago)

Text 18 was issued by Samuel Clay, Constable of Huddersfield in 1824 and again comes from the Huddersfield Archive. In it, he is asking the public for help with the enforcement and maintenance of law and order. His problem was that the police force in Huddersfield at that time consisted of . . . Samuel Clay . . . oh and his worthy assistant. If any major strife broke out, he had to call in the army or the militia. The militia were troops raised by compulsory ballot from the local people. They could not be sent abroad like the army but were used to put down riots and unrest. I feel sure that you are on the verge of spotting the obvious problem with this system, a problem which led the magistrates to be very wary of using the militia. When they were sent into action, they were more likely to join in with the rioters than throw them in prison, as they were very probably related to them. So, in the light of this, Samuel's task seems a thankless one and it gives this plea for help a certain appeal.

ACTIVITY 26

1 In groups, translate the poster into modern language and list the offences it is seeking to prevent.

2 Write the text for a modern equivalent, adding in any contemporary offences you feel are relevant, such as drug dealing, and updating as needed. Note the changes you have made.

3 As a whole group, discuss the social developments which have lead to these new crimes, then broaden out to all hi-tech treachery that the police have to cope with today. This should throw up a host of new words and phrases which you could use to discuss language change – *hacking* (as in computers) or *ringing* (as in cars). See how many you can come up with.

TEXT 26

genetic engineering

THE NEW RENAULT LAGUNA.

Humans have no need to evolve any more. Instead the things we create evolve for us. Our buildings, our computers and our brand new multivalve engines from the 100 bhp 1.6 16V to the 194 bhp 3.0 V6 24V and including a 100 bhp 1.9 direct injection cars change, adapt and improve at a rate that Darwin never dreamed possible. The new Renault Laguna is a shining example. turbo diesel. "Refined yet aurally delicious .... (as Autocar put it) with a creamy snarl...pulls with deceptive vigour."

A look under that sleek, sculpted skin will reveal an impressive genetic line leading directly to the BTCC winning Williams- Of course, the new Laguna has adapted to its own environment by developing smooth attractive styling, a sumptuous interior engineered Laguna. Survival (and success) in the BTCC environment, requires awesome power from the minimum weight with CD player and ABS as standard, air-conditioning and electric sunroof on most models and alist of safety features that coupled with astonishing reliability qualities that have been handed down to the new Laguna in the form of a range of many manufactures are struggling to match. Not to mention a staring price of just £13,570 on the road. Natural selection? Of course it is. To find out more telephone 0800 525150. **IT'S EVOLVED.**

RENAULT

1 Make two lists of the selling points for each respective car. Are there any crossing points? What would each audience be looking for in the new car? Profile the buyers.

2 What are the main similarities and differences between the ads? Which linguistic area shows the most change, in your view?

3 Discuss as a whole group the connotations of the brand names? Would you want to drive around in a 'Bean'? Why does it not work for us? Why does 'Laguna'? Or does it? Pool all the car names in your family etc and include them in your discussion. These cars were also marketed in the past:

- the Hupmobile (1920s)
- the Midget (1960s)
- the Messerschmidt (otherwise known as the Bubble car – 1960s)
- the Ford Prefect (late 1950s)
- the Ruby (1930s)
- the Legalimit (1900s)
- the Silent Rogue (1900s)

Compare with these contemporary brands:

- Orion
- Grand Vitara
- Quattro
- Shuttle
- Xantia
- Zetec.

She obviously doesn't use ... on her whites ...

From looking at these examples of texts, some patterns may be emerging, although the sample is small. There are similarities and differences in each of the pairings, but the process is much the same. What has changed is the social setting which gave rise to the ads and the attitudes which go hand in hand with that. This has led to the differences in form. Some of these are immediately recognisable as production techniques (you can tell a wartime ad just by looking at the images and graphology).

The audiences for products change as their circumstances change. 'Advertising is found in societies which have passed the point of satisfying the basic animal needs', said Marion Harper in the *New York Herald Tribune* 1960. Cures for the plague cannot be compared with the towel with the wings or the razor with the bendy head. As our existence has become more cushioned, the advertiser has had to fight harder to find corner of exclusivity in the market. Compare Ford's 'any colour as long as it's black' with the features offered by the Laguna ad. The *product* has changed, the *audience needs* have changed and so the *form* of the ads has changed. However, the basic purpose is the same – to make the buyer realise that s/he is dissatisfied and miraculously mend the problem by buying the product. This is what has become much trickier in this century.

The search for exclusivity is signalled in Mrs Vincent's ad, with her personal signature on each bottle. Later the patented brand name sealed a product forever as 'The Real Thing'. Very early ads, like the face soap, state the product and make large claims for it. By the 1920s, in a crowded market, social status was often attached to the product, as in the Parkinson Suburbia, with the added threat of social pariahship if you didn't use a particular brand. Recent ads have developed a sophisticated battery of

Everything you need available in store...

The purpose of an instruction is to enable the reader to carry out a set of actions efficiently. Thus, any written instruction must be crystal clear with no unnecessary wordiness. When giving spoken instructions, you would usually use gestures and demonstrate what it is you want people to do. To be as effective, the written version would need to be supported by diagrams and images to take the pressure off the words. A crisp partnership between words and visuals is essential for ease of understanding.

In the case of the recipe, the language structures are so well trodden, that everyone recognises it as a familiar **register**, leaving little room for confusion. However, the other job the modern recipe must do in today's crowded market, is to get attention. If you think of the supermarket as a huge food iceberg, then think of the recipe you can pick up at the checkout as the visible tip (and all the ingredients are coincidentally sold in the store!). Fancy ingredients may be the stock-in-trade of your modern TV chef – Ainsley Harriott, Ross Burden, Gary Rhodes, Delia Smith, Ken Hom. There are huge pressures to sell the ingredients, books, videos, cakes (Jane Asher) in the modern market place. In a way, these programmes are the electronic version of the old market trader shouting 'Luscious greens, go lovely with yer chops', but in recent years, the demands and lifestyles of the audience have changed in all sorts of ways.

Recipes have been around since written records began. One of the oldest dates from the Roman, first century and was supposedly written by the gourmet Apicius, who, on hearing that he had lost money and could not afford to uphold his gastronaut lifestyle, did the only honourable thing and poisoned himself. These early recipes differed from the present day versions in that they did not specify quantities and are therefore hard to reproduce today. Also, the ingredients are unfamiliar. Consider this handy recipe for *liquamen* (a spicy fish sauce favoured by the Romans):

'Take brine and test its strength by throwing an egg into it to try if it floats; if it sinks the brine does not contain enough salt. Put the fish into the brine in a new earthenware pot, add oregano, put it on a good fire till it boils.... Let it cool and strain it two or three times, until it is clear'.

(as quoted by Reay Tannahill in *Food in History* p 83)

Some recipe books survive from medieval times, but they all came from the kitchens of the rich. They still are vague about quantities (and continued to be so up to the fifteenth century) and were often written by royal cooks for themselves or their helpers, and not for an external market, as now. It was only in the nineteenth century that cookbooks became more accessible to the public, because of the wider spread of literacy. As food began to be used increasingly as a statement of wealth and position, cooks were often not up to the job, and the mistress of the house would turn to the recipe writers, among whom Isabella Beeton was the guiding light with her first edition in 1861. However, again, publishers targeted the middle classes and the books were out of reach of the working poor, who could afford neither the ingredients or the fuel to cook with. With increased prosperity and a welfare state to ensure minimum standards, only now in this century can most of us afford to go to buy pre-packed, canned, frozen foods at the local supermarket and choose from a bewildering array of ingredients to suit every purse.

ACTIVITY 34

1 Go to your local supermarkets and collect as many recipe cards as you can. Analyse the content of your data. How far are they informative and how far persuasive? Are they just aiming to sell ingredients? Are they particularly unusual? How does each store approach its customers. Analyse the consumer they seem to be aiming at? How does the language achieve its purpose? You are into the area of *language and power* here, the subject of another book in this series, which would make useful background reading for a project of this kind.

2 You could also look at the ready-prepared meals in a big supermarket (Marks and Spenser or Sainsburys) for ingredients, styles and origins.

'Take one chef...'

There are enough 'restaurants' today for us all to have one each, but you still can't get a booking when you want one, it seems. If they are all run by chefs, there must be training schools pumping them out like oil slicks. This does not appear to be the case, so what is happening? Look at this definition of a chef's abilities by A. A. Gill, food writer for *The Sunday Times*:

'Take a chef, any chef, and consider him. What does he need to know? Well, he needs to know physics, chemistry, biology, thermodynamics, engineering, prestidigitation and basic surgery. Whereas a doctor only has to know surgery on one species, a cook has to have a working knowledge of a couple of dozen: mammal, avian and piscatorial, not counting assorted bivalves, crustaceans and things with exoskeletons. And then there's vegetables. And fruit. And herbs and spices. And minerals and distillations. And oils. And gelatine. And enough recipes to make a lawyer's library look like an under-five's reading shelf. And he needs to know 'How do you do?' in three or four languages, plus a lexicon of technical terms. All of this before he's even a good chef.

To be a good chef, he needs artistry, design, imagination – oh, and I haven't mentioned taste. He has to have taste, in both senses. Now consider that anyone who wants to be a chef will, ipso facto, have an IQ on a par with that of a radish, the ambition of lard and the social skills of squid ink, and it's a blessed miracle that there are any chefs at all.'

(*Style*, 28 June 1998)

This sounds remarkably similar to Mrs Beeton's vision of the cook as a 'great personage' who gave orders from a high chair and beat his subordinates with a wooden spoon if they did not please him (*Book of Household Management*, page 37). So how is all this food being prepared? The work, which was done by the cook, in each household hierarchy is now done by individuals at home or by workers filling a market need for food. Gill calls them 'assemblers', practising a sort of cooking by numbers,

Muscatels	8d. to 1s. per lb.	Orange Pekoe	2s. 8d. per lb.
Spices, various	4½d. per tin.	Gunpowder	3s. per lb.
Sugar – Demerara	2½d. per lb.	Assam Pekoe	2s. 6d. per lb.
Loaf	2½d. per lb.	Oolong	2s. 6d. per lb.
Tea –		Young Hyson	2s. 6d. per lb.
Congou	1s. 2d. per lb.	Consolidated	2s. 8d. per lb.
Ceylon	1s. 6d. to 3s. per lb.	Yeast Powder	4d. per tin.

TEXT 30

LARGER INGREDIENTS USED ON
READY STEADY COOK

Arrowroot
Baking powder
Balsamic vinegar
Bay leaves
Beef stock cubes
Bottle of red wine
Bottle of white wine
Cardamom pods
Caster sugar
Cayenne pepper
Chicken stock cubes
Chilli powder
Clear honey
Cocoa powder
Cornflour
Demerara sugar
Dijon mustard
Double cream
Dried mixed herbs
Dried oregano
Eggs, size 3
Fresh basil
Fresh chervil

Fresh chives
Fresh coriander
Fresh dill
Fresh mint
Fresh parsley
Fresh rosemary
Fresh sage
Fresh thyme
Fresh white bread
Garam masala
Garlic
Golden syrup
Granulated sugar
Greek yoghurt
Ground all-spice
Ground cinnamon
Ground coriander
Ground cumin
Ground ginger
Ground nutmeg
Icing sugar
Lemons/limes
Milk

Olive oil
Oranges
Paprika
Peppercorns
Plain flour
Red-wine vinegar
Salt
Self-raising flour
Sesame oil
Soft brown sugar
Soy sauce
Sunflower oil
Tabasco sauce
Tomato purée
Tomato sauce
Turmeric
Unsalted butter
Vegetable stock cubes
Vanilla essence
Vanilla pod
White-wine vinegar
Wholegrain mustard
Worcestershire sauce

ACTIVITY 37

1 Find the origins of all the foodstuffs in both lists. Mrs Beeton says of 'Colonial and Foreign Cookery' on page vii of her preface:

'Britons living under other skies may learn how to combine the dishes of their adopted country with those of the Motherland. We at home may also gain variety in our own menus, and learn how to give complimentary and characteristic repast when welcoming guests from abroad.'

2 She mentions the Colonies often and the pattern of food imports will no doubt reflect a pattern of acquisitions from those countries. Using two, blank, world maps, mark on all the points of origin of each set of ingredients. To extend this, you could explore other old cookery books for supporting evidence and examine the foods available at a specific point in history

compared with now (go back and remind yourself of the table setting in Chapter 2 and the items shown there). Lexical borrowing has gone on throughout history, and food borrowings have ebbed and flowed with the movements of people. You could look at the major movements of people in this country in this century and look at the lexis which came with them, for example, the windrush of Caribbean settlers in the 1950s, the immigration of people from the Asian subcontinent, or alternatively explore the inrush of food lexis from America via the media and international travel (The Birth of the British Burger! The History of the Chip).

Ingredients of recipes – a shopping list

It is about time we looked at what actually makes up a recipe. You will immediately recognise one by its most obvious feature – the form of its verb, known as the imperative.

1 The imperative uses the base form of the verb and is used to make requests or commands. It is the main and most easily recognised feature of instructional writing. Functions of language are divided into different moods according to the purpose the utterance is being used for, for example, telling, asking, requesting or commanding. Each mood has a different structure:

■ 'The chef roasted the pheasant' = declarative mood – it is telling. The structure is Subject Verb Object
■ 'Did the chef roast the pheasant?' = interrogative mood – is asking. The structure is Auxiliary Verb (*did*) Subject Verb Object
■ 'Roast the pheasant' = imperative mood – it is requesting or commanding. The structure is Verb Object with no subject, although it could appear as the named person who is being ordered to do the action ('Roast the pheasant, chef'). In a recipe, the subject would, of course, be you, the reader.

2 The structure of a recipe is, therefore, usually a string of imperative sentences, consisting of VO structures.

3 The irritability rating of the command can be varied by use of modal auxiliaries. Take these two examples:

■ 'Grate chocolate over the gateau'
■ 'You *could* grate chocolate over the gateau.'

Modals are a group of auxiliary verbs (helping verbs) which signal modality, that is, not hard fact, but the potential for something being done. The potential of grating the chocolate is clearly referred to in the second example, but not in the first. The tone of a recipe can be very different when modals are inserted. However, note that the grammatical structure is the same.

lexical and grammatical features, which add up to the overall effect. You could, for example, immediately spot the register of the tabloid newspaper, complete with emotive words, minor sentences and puns. Or you would recognise a text book register, perhaps science, with questions, declarative sentences and scientific lexis.

RUNES The system of writing which had been used by the early Germanic peoples from at least 300 AD. They are thought to come originally from a Greek alphabet. They were angular in form as they were generally carved onto trees, metal objects or stone. Many carved crosses still survive in Northumberland today with runic inscriptions. 'Rune' meant 'secret' and they were thought, at one time, to have magical powers. Some runic symbols were added to the Roman alphabet, which we use today, by Anglo Saxon scribes, to cover sounds they were not familiar with. These were 'ash,' 'thorn' and 'wynn'. An enjoyable way to explore runes would be to read *The Lord Of The Rings* by J.R.R. Tolkein.

SEMANTICS The study of word meanings.

SEMANTIC SHIFT When a word adopts a slightly different meaning, or a definite change, for example, a 'mouse' used to be a small furry animal but now has developed a second meaning as the controller on a computer.

SLANG One of the factories of language change, which churns out new words at a rapid rate. Slang is the 'bargain basement' of language, where users rummage about to see if anything is worth keeping, and discard the rest. Slang is new, fresh and usually very aggressive. It often offends and is used by groups to give themselves an identity. Slang is a fertile source of lexical change. Look at the numerous slang dictionaries on the market, particularly the introductions, which give you all sorts of useful titbits for essays.

STANDARD ENGLISH The dialect of English which is associated with education and class. It is used in textbooks, education and is taught to foreign learners. It is known by most people as the type of language used by the BBC. It was adopted by Lord Reith in 1922 as a variety which could be understood by all and not laughed at by anyone.

STANDARDISATION The process of moving from a situation where everyone spoke and wrote in their own individual fashion, to the present day, when we all use the common variety of standard English to communicate to wider audiences. The process has been going on for centuries, but accelerated at particular points in history, such as the introduction of the printing process by Caxton in 1476 and the development of widescale dictionaries in the eighteenth century. Standardisation is being strongly reinforced today by factors such as computing, international media and educational policies.

SYNTAX (INVERTED) Syntax is another name for the ordering of words in a sentence, according to the rules which govern language. One of the most basic syntactic rules in English is that the subject comes first and is followed by the verb. When syntactic rules are inverted, it means that the order is reversed. This is a common feature of language from earlier periods when word order was not as rigid as it is now.